SERIOUSLY

SILLY
JOKES

THE BEANO books
geddes & grosset

4

5

6

7

8

9

13

What do you get if you cross Roger with a timepiece?
A dodge-it-all watch!

What's brown and can see just as well from either end?
A horse with its eyes closed.

15

What's orange, hairy and comes back to you?
A
boomerangutang.

What did the Spaniard say to his hen?
O, lay!

What's a monster's favourite game?
Corpse and robbers!

What do Italian ghosts have for tea?
Spooketti!

What did the vampire say to his girlfriend?
After the film, do you fancy a bite?

What fiend ate too much porridge?
Ghouldilocks!

What do you call
a Spaniard
leaving hospital?
Manwell!

What do you call
a Spaniard
who's had his
vehicle stolen?
Carlos!

What do you get if you cross a chicken with a guitar? A bird that makes music when you pluck it!

Why didn't the shark eat the woman who fell overboard? 'Cos it was a MAN eating shark!

What do you do with a green sea monster? Wait till it ripens!

What swims and goes 'click'? A ball point fish!

What do spacemen play
on their way to the
moon?
*Astronauts and
crosses.*

Did you hear about the man
who put his false teeth in
backwards?
He ate himself!

What happened to the girl
who slept with her head
under the pillow?
*The tooth fairy took all
her teeth!*

Who throws boomerangs and
comes from another planet?
An Australien!

25

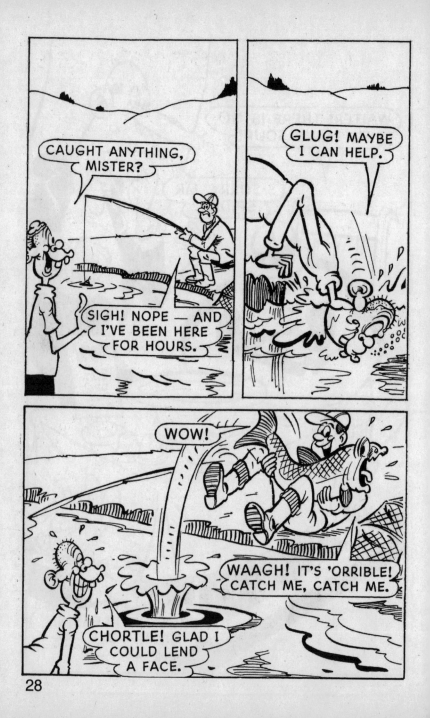

FAMOUS LAST WORDS!

31

35

37

What do you get if you cross a snake with a glow worm? A three metre long strip light!

My wooden leg hurts.
How?
My wife hits me with it.

Doctor — I keep thinking I'm a rough sea.
Calm down man!

Why do elephants have red eyes?
So they can hide in cherry trees.

Have you ever seen an elephant
in a cherry tree?
No — Shows how well they're
hidden, eh?

How did the
farmer get
squashed?
Dunno!
He went
cherry picking,
of course!

How d'you know there's an elephant in your cherry tree?

When two of the cherries wear sunglasses on sunny days.

What do you get if you cross a compact disc with a fridge?

Very cool music!

Where do aliens go to study? Mooniversity!

What do cats eat for breakfast? Mice krispies!

41

What do you get if you cross a cow with a camel?
Lumpy milk-shakes.

What do you call a cow that doesn't give milk?
An UDDER failure!

What would happen if cows could fly?
The price of beef would go up and you'd get lots of pats on the head.

43

Did you hear about the sick spy?
He had a CODE in his nose.

What's yellow, soft and goes round and round?
A long playing omelette!

Who lost a herd of elephants?
BIG BO PEEP!

Who invented
flavoured crisps?
Sultan Vinegar!

What do monsters
eat in restaurants?
The waiter!

What do you
call a
three-sided
frying pan?
A friangle!

46

What does it mean when you find a set of horse-shoes? There's a horse going around in its socks!

48

Right, m'lad, I want you to accompany me to the police station.
B-but, what have I d-done wrong?
Nothing! But I get so frightened on my own with all those nasty people around.

What do you get if you cross an elephant with a sparrow? Broken telephone wires!

53

55

56

58

59

Did you hear about the two deer who ran away to get married?
They antELOPED!

What did the father buffalo say to his youngster when he went to school?
BI SON!

What can you see through that has eight legs? A black WINDOW spider!

What do you do about fighting snails? Let them slug it out!

What do you get if you cross a centipede with a turkey? Drumsticks for everyone!

Where does a forty stone gorilla sit in the cinema? ANYWHERE IT LIKES!

What did the ghost teacher say to his class?
It's ghoul time!

What games do ghosts like to play?
Haunt the thimble and hide and shriek!

What do you call a kind, handsome loveable monster?
A FAILURE!

Don't keep reaching for the food.
Haven't you got a tongue?
Yes! But my arms are longer!

Two vegetables got married . . .
. . . they exchanged onion rings!

Why did Henry VIII have so many wives? 'Cos he liked to chop and change!

Why did the skeleton go to the restaurant?
He wanted spare ribs!

What do you get when you cross a hyena with a beef cube!
A laughing stock!

How do you communicate with fish?
Drop them a line.

What fish swims only at night?
A starfish.

What's the biggest moth?
A mamMOTH!

How do dinosaurs pass exams?
With EXTINCTION!

81

82

85

The best time to take a bath is just before you retire. Great! I won't have to have one till I'm sixty-five!

Er — I was going to buy a handkerchief for your birthday . . . but I forgot the size of your nose.

How many silly electricians does it take to change a lightbulb?
A hundred and one — one to hold the bulb and a hundred to turn the house round!

What's green, got 6 legs and if it falls out of a tree will kill you?
A snooker table.

Where do dogs keep their money?
Barklay's Bank.

Where do you find a tortoise with no legs? Where you left it.

What do polite mice say? Cheese and thank you!

**What room has no walls,
floor, ceiling or windows.
A mushroom.**

**What has a neck
but no head?
A bottle.**

**Why are Brownies dizzy?
Because they are always
doing good turns!**

**Why did Smiffy park his bike
by his bed?
He was fed up sleepwalking.**

Doctor, doctor. Every time I drink a cup of hot tea, I get a pain in my eye.
Try taking the spoon out.

Why is it useless telling shopkeepers to be quiet?
Because they don't shut up till the end of the day.